Scholarships for Average Students

Key Strategies to Help High School and College Students Win Scholarship Money Without Top Grades

Also by Marianne Ragins

Winning Scholarships for College
College Survival & Success Skills 101
Senior Year Head Start

Scholarships *for* Average Students

Key Strategies to Help High School and College Students Win Scholarship Money *Without* Top Grades

Marianne Ragins

TSW Publishing
P. O. Box 176
Centreville, Virginia 20122
www.scholarshipworkshop.com
TSW Publishing is a division of The Scholarship Workshop LLC

Copyright © 2025 by Marianne Ragins
All rights reserved. No part of this book may be used or reproduced in any manner whatsoever without prior written consent of the author, except as provided by the United States of America copyright law.

Scholarships for Average Students was written to provide accurate advice to readers. However, please note that the author nor the publisher are engaged in the practice of providing legal, accounting, tax or other professional advice unless otherwise indicated. If you need legal, accounting, tax or other advice, please consult a professional in the appropriate area. Neither the author, the publisher, nor any entity associated with *Scholarships for Average Students* assume any liability for errors, omissions, or inaccuracies. Any action you take or do not take as a result of reading *Scholarships for Average Students* is entirely your responsibility.

ISBN: 978-1-950653-27-0

Printed in the United States of America

This book is available at special quantity discounts for bulk purchases for sales promotions, premiums, fundraising, and educational use. Special versions or book excerpts can also be created to fit specific needs.

For more information, please contact info@scholarshipworkshop.com or call 703 579-4245. You can also write: TSW Publishing, P. O. Box 176, Centreville, Virginia 20122.

Dedication

To my mother, my husband and my teens; your love, motivation, and presence in my life keep me going.

For G. L. Solomon
As one who truly got the most from life
and helped us to get the most from ours,
your sunny smile, loving heart and
generous ways will be remembered forever
by all of your family and friends.

Contents

Introduction 11

Finding Specific Scholarships Average Students Can Win 14

Exploring Scholarships, Awards and Prizes for Average Students 23

Easy Scholarships for Lucky Average Students 49

Earning Scholarships for Activities You Complete, Not Your GPA 55

Searching for Additional Scholarships 58

Applications 67

Essential Application Tools to Help You Win 69

Essay Writing Tips to Help Average Students Win 76

Scholarships Hacks and Mistakes To Avoid 83

Other Strategies to Reduce Your Tuition Bills 87

Using Crowdfunding to Get Money for College ... 90

Introduction

Can students without top grades or "A" averages win scholarships? Yes! They can undoubtedly win college scholarships. Having an "A" average can help you win scholarships, but many scholarships may not require an "A" grade point average (GPA), or the requirement for a GPA may be a 3.0 or lower. This is because merit goes beyond achieving the highest grades in the classroom. It can include your activities beyond the classroom as well. So, if you can achieve a "B" average, you can qualify for most scholarships. Also, be proud of yourself! A "B" average is terrific and still an excellent GPA. With so many honors/advanced, Advanced Placement (AP), and Dual Enrollment (DE) courses available in many school systems that could increase a student's GPA beyond a 4.0, it can be challenging to stand out, even though a "B" average means you have performed well in the classroom. Also, even if you don't have a 3.0 GPA, you still have opportunities—essay contests, artistic contests, video contests, and even contests based on social media and texting—that do not require information about your grades. In addition, if you're involved in your community, many programs are also impressed by your service to others and the volunteer aspects listed in your student activities résumé. See chapter 14 in the sixth or later edition of *Winning Scholarships for*

Scholarships for Average Students

College, "Scholarships and Awards for Community Service, Volunteering, and Work."

It is important to remember that most scholarship programs including those at colleges and universities are looking for well-rounded students. They want students who not only perform well in the classroom but excel beyond academics. What does this mean? If you've been involved in leadership activities, community activities, special hobbies, athletic activities, tutoring, mentoring, or even show an awareness of important global and social issues and how you might positively influence the world, you can impress a scholarship program. If you can showcase your activities and your potential, you have a great chance to win scholarships. So don't let your less-than-stellar grades discourage you. And don't let test scores discourage you, either, because there are many scholarship programs that do not request specific test scores. This includes merit scholarship programs at colleges and universities as well as those sponsored by associations, foundations, clubs, fraternities, sororities and many other types of organizations.

However, don't think I'm telling you that grades and test scores do not matter in winning scholarships. You do need to make every attempt to get your grades and test scores as high as possible. However, even if you don't achieve an "A" or even a "B," there are still scholarships that might be right for you. This book will help you uncover these opportunities.

Keep reading for examples of scholarships, awards, and prizes you can win even without an "A" average. Remember, these are to give you a jumpstart. There are many opportunities that may go beyond this publication.

Overall, successful, organized students should apply for all scholarships for which they are eligible. Look for merit scholarships, awards, contests, and competitions that do not require a 4.0 or higher GPA, or don't ask for information about your grades.

1

Finding Specific Scholarships Average Students Can Win

One crucial area to explore for scholarships is those specific to you, your circumstances and interests, your background, and your family. Start exploring specific scholarships in these areas by asking yourself the following questions:

Where do you live? Have you checked for community foundations in your area?

Organizations and companies offer scholarships to students who live in a specific area, usually where the company or organization is located or does business. To find scholarships in this category, do an advanced Internet search to find community foundations, county websites, or school websites with scholarships specific to your area. Use search terms such as "scholarships" and the name of your county, city, or state to find scholarships in local areas. Also, do the same for "scholarships" and search for the word "community foundation" along with the name of your city, county, or state to uncover community foundations in your area. For example, the Community Foundation of Northern Virginia (https://www.cfnova.org), the Berks County

1 – Finding Specific Scholarships

Community Foundation in Pennsylvania (http://www.bccf.org), and the Community Foundation of Central Georgia (http://www.cfcga.org) are all examples of community-based foundations that serve a specific community or a group of communities within a specific region.

What are your extracurricular activities?
Activities such as participation in Distributive Education Club of America (DECA; http://www.deca.org), Future Business Leaders of America (FBLA; http://www.fbla-pbl.org), the National Honor Society (NHS; http://www.nhs.us), and Junior Achievement (http://www.ja.org) may allow you to become eligible for scholarships from these organizations or as members of these organizations. For example, high school seniors who are members of DECA are eligible for renewable Harry A. Applegate Scholarships, for use in pursuing business education.

What are your hobbies?
There are many scholarships for people who have particular hobbies. Books with extensive scholarship listings will have special sections dealing with these types of scholarships. Look for these special sections during your scholarship search. Some scholarship directories will title this section as extracurricular activities. An example of a scholarship or award that focuses on your hobbies would be the Pokémon World Championships (https://www.pokemon.com/us/play-pokemon

—see *World Championships*). Players can win up to $25,000 in scholarships or cash.

If you are currently employed, where do you work? Contact the personnel or human resources office of your employer to inquire about scholarship opportunities and tuition reimbursement programs. If your company does not have a personnel office, speak with the general manager about the possibility of scholarship opportunities, or contact the company's general headquarters to learn if such opportunities exist. Many companies offer tuition reimbursement programs as an employee benefit. In tuition reimbursement, the employee initially pays the cost of tuition and fees for the courses taken in college or graduate school. Once the courses are completed and a satisfactory grade has been earned by the employee, the company/employer will then reimburse all or part of the tuition and fees initially paid by the employee. Some companies pay these costs upfront. As a student working at Wendy's Old-Fashioned Hamburgers in high school, I was eligible for a Wendy's scholarship which I applied for and won.

For what company or companies do your parents currently work?

Ask your parents to contact their company personnel or human resources department to inquire if there are scholarships available to the

1 – Finding Specific Scholarships

children of employees. If the company does not have a personnel office, your parent should speak with the general manager about the possibility of scholarship opportunities or contact the company's general headquarters. Scholarship directories also list companies that sponsor scholarship programs for the children of their employees. You can also check books or online directories such as *The Foundation Directory Online* (https://fconline.foundationcenter.org), to learn whether your parent's company has a foundation set up to disburse scholarship money to the children of their employees or for other purposes. For example, Johnson Controls, Inc., maintains the Johnson Controls Foundation that offers scholarships to its employees' children.

Do you belong to a religious organization; for example, a church or synagogue?

Many religious organizations give scholarships not only to members of their congregations but to nonmembers as well. Some of them stipulate that the recipients of their scholarships must attend a college or university established to operate under the edicts of their denominational faith, such as a Presbyterian college or university. An example of this type of scholarship would be the Presbyterian Scholarships (http://www.presbyterianmission.org) offered to students who are members of the Presbyterian Church and are planning to attend a college related to the Presbyterian Church (U.S.A). Contact churches and religious organizations to inquire

Scholarships for Average Students

about scholarships such as these. You can also look in scholarship directories for the sections based on religious affiliations. In addition, speak with the minister of the church that either you and/or your parents attend. Most churches are more than willing to establish a small scholarship fund for their students. For instance, the church I was a member of in Macon, Georgia, Stubbs Chapel Baptist Church, gave me a small scholarship to attend college and also gave me money every year while I was enrolled.

Are you a child or close relative of a war veteran? If so, in which war and in what branch of service did your relative serve?

Numerous scholarships are available for children and close relatives of veterans who served in specific wars, such as World War II. Books with extensive scholarship listings will have special sections dealing with these types of scholarships. The sections may be titled "Armed Forces" or "Military." You will need to know the branch of the Armed Forces in which your relative served to find scholarships that apply specifically to you. Examples of these scholarships are those offered by the Military Benefit Association, which provides scholarships to its members who serve in the military (http://www.militarybenefit.org). The Fisher House Foundation's website (http://www.militaryscholar.org) is another resource for scholarship information associated with the military.

1 – Finding Specific Scholarships

Are you a veteran or a disabled veteran?
Scholarship and financial assistance is available to most disabled veterans, especially from the government. If you are a disabled veteran, contact the Federal Student Aid Information Center (800-433-3243), visit StudentAid.gov to inquire about scholarship opportunities, or call the Department of Veterans Affairs (800-827-1000; http://www.va.gov or http://www.gibill.va.gov). You may find governmental organizations with programs that pay for tuition, fees, books, and equipment of veterans disabled during active duty and honorably discharged. To find financial aid such as this, look in the "Military Disabled" or "Armed Forces" sections of the scholarship guides.

Are you legally blind or do you have any other disabilities?
Students who are legally blind or in some other way disabled can usually receive scholarships and financial aid assistance from many sources, especially the government. During your search, look for directories that have special sections dealing with scholarships for the disabled. The American Council of the Blind (http://www.acb.org) currently offers scholarships to students who are legally blind.

Are you related to someone with a disability or who is a survivor of a disease?

Scholarships for Average Students

For example, if your parent is deaf or hard-of-hearing, the Millie Brother Scholarship for Hearing Children of Deaf Adults is offered through Children of Deaf Adults (CODA) (www.coda-international.org). There are also scholarships for survivors of certain diseases such as cancer. Currently the Dr. Angela Grant Memorial Scholarship Fund awards scholarships to cancer survivors or those within the immediate family of a cancer survivor (http://www.drangelagrantscholarship.org). This is an area where an advanced Internet search, could be helpful to you in finding college aid specific to your situation, disease, or disability.

For minority groups other than African American, can you trace your lineage? (For example, Samoan, Japanese, Native American, etc.)

Many programs have scholarships strictly for minorities of a certain descent. To win these scholarships you may be required to prove your lineage. Look for scholarships such as these if you fall into this category. An example of this type of scholarship would be the scholarships offered by the Welsh Society of Philadelphia to students of Welsh descent (http://www.philadelphiawelsh.org). To be eligible to receive this scholarship, applicants must prove their lineage and enroll in a college within 100 miles of Philadelphia.

Are you or your parents a member of a union, trade group, or association?

1 – Finding Specific Scholarships

If you or your parents are members of a union, trade group, or association, you may be eligible to win scholarships such as the E. C. Hallbeck Memorial Scholarship offered by the American Postal Workers Union (http://www.apwu.org) to high school seniors who are dependents of active or deceased members of the union. Or consider the scholarship program from Union Plus (http://www.unionplus.org), an organization established by the AFL- CIO to provide consumer benefits to members and retirees of participating labor unions.

What are you strongly interested in studying at college? Scholarships are available to students interested in a particular major. If you are certain of your intended major, look for directories and scholarship opportunities in that area. For students interested in the field of health care, for example, the Tylenol Future Care Scholarship program (https://www.tylenol.com/news/scholarship) is available, or consider reviewing scholarships offered by the American Medical Association Foundation (http://www.ama-assn.org). The scholarships don't just stop at health care or medicine—you can find other associations for scholarships in other fields. Use a scholarship directory or perform an advanced Internet search to find scholarships related to your current or future major.

Are you a member of a fraternity or sorority? Many sororities and fraternities sponsor scholarships. For instance, members of Theta Delta

Scholarships for Average Students

Chi can apply for scholarships, and the Alpha Kappa Alpha Sorority, Inc., Educational Advancement Foundation also offers several scholarships, including some that are open to nonmembers. As you look through scholarship directories, look for scholarships sponsored by a fraternity or sorority. If you are unable to discover any, write or call the national chapter of your organization, or visit its website, Facebook, or other social media platforms to uncover opportunities. In fact, local sororities and fraternities will often contact me (author of this book) to help them advertise a scholarship program that may be suffering from a low application rate.

Are your parents' members of a fraternity or sorority? Some sororities and fraternities sponsor scholarships for the children of their members. As you look through scholarship directories, look for scholarships sponsored by your parents' fraternity or sorority. If you are unable to discover any, write to the national chapters of the organizations or visit their website, Facebook, Instagram, or other social media platforms, if available. You can also do an advanced Internet search.

Are your parents' alumni of a college or university? Many colleges and universities offer scholarships to the children of their alumni. Contact the college or university they attended to inquire about scholarship opportunities that may be available to you.

2

Exploring Scholarships, Awards and Prizes for Average Students

This chapter will help you explore general scholarships, awards, and prizes that students without top grades can apply for and win. These college money sources can be used for most majors and career fields and a variety of students are eligible to apply for them. Please contact each organization to confirm or update deadlines and eligibility criteria. Under no circumstances should you use this listing as the sole resource for your scholarship search. The purpose of this publication is to help you find scholarships that are specific to your situation and to show you steps to help you win them. The provision of the following list of scholarships is meant only to give you a jump-start on the scholarship process.

Remember! College money can also be available as prize winnings for art, writing, speaking or other talent contests such as the *American Legion National High School Oratorical Contest* and the *Doodle 4 Google* contest. Or, the money is associated with outstanding community service such as the *Jesse Brown Memorial Youth*

Scholarships for Average Students

Scholarship Program. Too, there are scholarships associated with promoting certain behavior, such as the *Project Yellow Light/Hunter Garner Scholarship* where students focus on efforts to promote safe driving habits.

If you're a parent reading this publication and you're grooming your son or daughter to have the best chances of getting scholarship or prize money to help with college early, encourage them to explore their creative and scientific side. Also help them to understand the importance of giving back. Participating in community service and exploration into potential special talents can help them win scholarships, awards, and prizes. This can boost their opportunities for free college money as a young student but also for scholarships as high school senior no matter where their GPA happens to be. Note: *Scholarships can be won as early as age 6.*

If you win a scholarship before you actually start your college studies, the money is usually held for you by the sponsoring organization. Once you notify the organization with information about your college or university, funds are often dispersed directly to the school. There are some awards you can win that are not technically considered scholarships and the funds may be sent directly to you immediately after you win. This information is normally included in the sponsor's program materials or website. If funds are remitted directly to you, save! Don't spend! Or, if necessary, the funds could be spent to help pay for a current

2 – Exploring Scholarships and Awards

year's private school tuition, if you believe the benefits of the money being used for private school now outweigh the benefits of helping to pay for college later.

A FEW IMPORTANT ITEMS TO REMEMBER

- Deadlines change frequently. For a scholarship program, prize, contest, or an award, visit the website or social media page listed to get the most recent information. Or you can review *The Scholarship Monthly Planner or* our website at://www.scholarshipworkshop.com. *The Scholarship Monthly Planner* includes frequently updated deadlines.
- Join us on Facebook and Instagram @ScholarshipWorkshop and X (formerly Twitter) @ScholarshipWork for updates via social media. You can also visit our website to sign up for our newsletter to receive the latest scholarship updates and other helpful information. Visit http://www.scholarshipworkshop.com/newsletter to get on our mailing list.
- Do not send blanket e-mails requesting an application from an organization. Many organizations have many people interested in their programs and may not respond.
- Some programs change their application requirements and eligibility guidelines. Please review their websites carefully for any changes.
- If you've reviewed their website thoroughly and still have questions, use the e-mail address and/or telephone number, if provided.
- Programs can and do stop awarding scholarships or suspend their scholarship programs. Don't get discouraged. You can still find available scholarships. But please know that there are no guarantees about the availability of a given scholarship, or that you will win it.

Scholarships for Average Students

American Fire Sprinkler Association Scholarship

Second Chance Scholarship Contest
Website: http://www.afsascholarship.org
Additional Information: Current college or trade school students can win $1,000 in the American Fire Sprinkler Association (AFSA) Second Chance Scholarship Contest. To enter, you must complete the registration page with all requested information. Then read the "Fire Sprinkler Essay" about automatic fire sprinklers and answer multiple choice questions in a short online test. After reading the information and answering the questions, you will get one entry into a drawing for one of five $1,000 scholarships.

American Legion National High School Oratorical Contest

Website: http://www.legion.org (click on *Programs\Family and Youth\Scholarships\Oratorical Contest*)
Additional Information: Open to students in grades 9 through 12 who are less than 20 years of age (as of the national contest deadline) and are U.S. citizens or lawful permanent residents of the United States. You must be currently enrolled in a high school or middle school (public, parochial, military, private, or state-accredited homeschool) in which the curriculum is considered to be of high school level. You must be able to prepare and deliver speeches in public to win these awards. In

addition to the scholarships awarded by the national headquarters, several hundred scholarships may be awarded by intermediate organizations to participants at the post, district, county, or department levels of competition. Visit the website for more details and current deadlines. Award amounts range from $2,000 to $25,000.

American Mensa Education and Research Foundation

E-mail: info@mensafoundation.org
Website: http://www.mensafoundation.org
Additional Information: Open to citizens or permanent residents of the United States. You must be planning to enroll for the academic year following the award in a degree program in an accredited American institution of post-secondary education. Awards are based totally on essays written by applicants. This organization does not require applicants to be Mensa members nor do they consider grades, academic program, or financial need when selecting applicants. Selection is based solely on an essay describing your career, vocational, and/or academic goals. Essay should be fewer than 550 words and must be specific rather than general. The essays are judged on content, grammar, organization, and craftsmanship. To get an online application, visit the website. Awards can be used for all fields of study. The deadline is usually January 15. Applications become available

online in September. Awards range from $500 to $2,500.

Ayn Rand's Novelette *Anthem* Essay Contest

E-mail: essays@aynrand.org
Website: http://www.aynrand.org/contests
Additional Information: Open to 8th, 9th, 10th, 11th and 12th grade students who submit an essay of 600 to 1,200 words. Awards range from $25 to $2,000.

Ayn Rand's Novel *The Fountainhead* Essay Contest

E-mail: essays@aynrand.org
Website: http://www.aynrand.org/contests
Additional Information: Open to 11th and 12th grade high school students who submit an essay of 800 to 1,600 words. Awards range from $25 to $5,000.

Burger King Scholars

Website: https://www.burgerkingfoundation.org (see *Burger King Scholars Program*) or https://burgerking.scholarsapply.org or https://bk-scholars.com
Additional Information: This scholarship is open to all high school seniors. All company and participating Burger King franchises as well as corporate and field employees and children of

2 – Exploring Scholarships and Awards

employees are also eligible. Scholarships range from $1,000 to $60,000, and are intended to help students in the United States, Puerto Rico and Canada offset the cost of attending college or post-secondary vocational/technical school. Awards are based on grade point average, work experience, extracurricular activities, and/or community service.

C-Span's Student Cam

Website: http://www.studentcam.org
Additional Information: StudentCam is an annual national video competition from C-SPAN that encourages students to think critically about issues that affect the nation and its communities. To enter this competition you must be in grades 6-12 and create a short (5-6 minute) video documentary on a topic related to the yearly competition theme. You can compete individually or in teams of either two or three members and your video documentary must include clips of supporting C-SPAN video relating to the topic. Up to $100,000 in cash prizes are awarded.

College Is Power Scholarship

Website:
http://www.collegeispower.com/scholarship.cfm

Scholarships for Average Students

Additional Information: This scholarship is available to students 17 years of age or older who plan to start a program of higher education within the next twelve months or who are currently enrolled in a program of higher education. You must be a full- or part-time student, attend a campus-based or online program and be a citizen or permanent resident of the United States. Award amount is $1,000.

College JumpStart Scholarship

Website: www.jumpstart-scholarship.net
Additional Information: This scholarship is open to 10th through 12th grade high school students, college students and non-traditional students who are U.S. citizens or legal residents. You must be attending or planning to attend an accredited 2-year, 4-year or vocational/trade school in the U.S. and be committed to using education to better your life and that of your family and/or community.

Courageous Persuaders

Website: http://courageouspersuaders.com
Additional Information: Students in grades 9 through 12 in teams or individually, can create commercials up to 30 seconds long about the dangers of underage drinking or the dangers of texting while driving. The commercials are intended for middle school audiences and will be

judged on originality, creativity and persuasiveness. Winners can receive up to $2,000 and students can enter separate videos in both categories.

Create-A-Greeting Card Scholarship Contest

Website: www.gallerycollection.com (Search for *Scholarship Contests*)

Additional Information: This $10,000 scholarship contest is open to all high school (at least 14 years of age or older) AND college students AND members of the armed forces who are enrolled during the time-period of the contest in an academic program designed to conclude with the awarding of a diploma or a degree. To participate, applicants must create a design for a Christmas card, holiday card, birthday card or all-occasion greeting card. Legal residents of the fifty (50) United States, the District of Columbia, American Samoa, Guam, the Commonwealth of the Northern Mariana Islands, the U.S. Virgin Islands, and Puerto Rico are eligible to enter. International students who have a student visa to attend school in the United States are considered legal residents and are also eligible to enter.

Create Real Impact Contest

Website: https://www.createrealimpact.com

Scholarships for Average Students

Additional Information: The Create Real Impact Scholarship provides monetary prizes of up to $1,500 for middle school, high school and college students between the ages of 14 and 22. To enter the contest, students are asked to showcase their positive solutions and strategies to stop the primary killer of young people: car crashes caused by reckless and distracted driving. Students can submit an entry into one of two categories: video or graphic design. Also, if students get local community champions involved, such as first responder agencies and elected officials, they earn another chance to win in the Community Champions Bonus Points category.

Doodle 4 Google

Website: http://www.google.com/doodle4google or https://doodles.google.com/d4g

Additional Information: Doodle 4 Google is an annual program that encourages K–12 students in the United States to use their artistic talents to think big and redesign the Google home page logo for millions to see. Previous themes have been "My Best Day Ever," "What I Want to Do Someday," and "What Inspires Me." Recently students were asked to use their imagination to create a Google Doodle based on what they're grateful for. Winning student artists will see their artwork appear on Google, receive a $30,000 college scholarship, and a $50,000 technology grant for

2 – Exploring Scholarships and Awards

their school, along with some other great prizes. Visit the website for complete eligibility guidelines, templates, and submission information.

DoSomething.Org Easy Scholarship Campaigns

Website: http://www.dosomething.org (see *Scholarships* section on the website).
Social Media: Follow DoSomething.org on Facebook (https://www.facebook.com/dosomething), Instagram @dosomething, and X (formerly Twitter) @dosomething
Additional Information: DoSomething.org is a nonprofit for young people focused on social change for causes such as bullying, homelessness, and cancer. To apply for a scholarship, you need to complete a campaign and prove it with pictures of you in action during the campaign. They have many campaigns featured on the website. The scholarship program is open to U.S. citizens between the ages 13 and 25 and does not require a minimum GPA.

Frame My Future Scholarship Contest

Website: http://www.diplomaframe.com (search for *"Frame My Future Scholarship Contest"*) or https://www.diplomaframe.com/contests/frame-my-future-scholarship.aspx

Scholarships for Average Students

Additional Information: This contest is open to U.S. citizens enrolled in community college, undergraduate, or graduate school attending a U.S. college or university full-time in the current academic year. To qualify, you must submit an original creation of poetry, photography, ink, collage, painting, mixed media, or graphic design to share what you want to achieve in your personal and professional life after college. Students can win up to $6,000. Finalists are judged based on their entry and description. Winners are ultimately chosen by online vote. For additional information and current deadline, visit the website.

The Gloria Barron Prize for Young Heroes

Website: https://barronprize.org
Additional Information: Each year, the Gloria Barron Prize for Young Heroes honors outstanding youth leaders ages 8 to 18 who have made a significant positive difference to people and the environment. Top winners in this program receive a $10,000 cash award to support their service work or higher education. The deadline is usually in April. Visit the website for additional information about references, application requirements and other details.

2 – Exploring Scholarships and Awards

Horatio Alger National Scholarship Program

Website: http://www.horatioalger.org or https://scholars.horatioalger.org or https://horatioalger.org/scholarships-and-services

Additional Information: The Horatio Alger National Scholarship Program is designed to help high school students who have faced and overcome great obstacles or adversities. The program also recognizes students who show academic achievement and leadership potential. To be eligible for this scholarship you must be enrolled full-time as a high school senior, progressing normally toward graduation, and planning to enter college no later than the fall following graduation. You must also have a strong commitment to pursue a bachelor's degree at an accredited institution (you can start your studies at a two-year institution and then transfer to a four-year institution); have critical financial need; be involved in extracurricular and community activities; have a minimum 2.0 GPA; and be a citizen of the United States. Scholarships are for $25,000 (payable over four years). and winners receive an all-expense-paid trip to Washington, D.C., during the spring of their senior year to participate in the National Scholars Conference.

Note: Please allow plenty of time to apply for this scholarship. In previous years, they have required four essays. One essay required you to compare your life with that of a Horatio Alger Association member, which means you should research the association and its members to plan and write your essay. The other essays involve the adversity or obstacles you've faced and overcome. Even if the contrast and comparison essay relating to a Horatio Alger Association member is no longer a requirement, I strongly suggest you do so anyway as part of your adversity essay to make it even stronger and to show you care enough about the organization and its mission to research its members.

Jesse Brown Memorial Youth Scholarship Program and DAV Scholarships

Website: http://www.dav.org (search *Scholarships* or *Jesse Brown Youth Memorial Scholarship*) or link to https://www.dav.org/get-involved/volunteer/dav-scholarships

Additional Information: The Jesse Brown Memorial Youth Scholarship Program was established to recognize youth volunteers age 21 or younger who have volunteered for a minimum of 100 hours at a DAV or DAV facility such as a VA medical center during the previous calendar year. You must be nominated for this program and write a 750-word essay titled "What Volunteering Has Meant to Me." You can also nominate yourself. See the website for additional eligibility criteria, current deadlines, and the nomination form. Scholarship amounts can be up to $30,000.

2 – Exploring Scholarships and Awards

"Leading the Future II" Scholarship

Website: http://www.scholarshipworkshop.com
Additional Information: The "Leading the Future" Scholarship is designed to elevate students' consciousness about their future and their role in helping others once they receive a college degree and become established in a community. It is open to high school seniors or current college undergraduates who are U.S. residents. Visit the website to apply online.

Live Más Scholarship

Website: https://www.tacobellfoundation.org/live-mas-scholarship
Additional Information: The Live Más Scholarship is open to college students who submit a video between 30 seconds and 2 minutes in length that addresses these questions:
- What is your passion and how are you currently pursuing it?
- How do you plan to use your passion to uniquely make a positive change in your community or the world?
- How will your education help enable you to pursue your passion and make a change?

You must be between 16 and 26 years in age and on-track to apply for or enrolled in an accredited post-high school/post-secondary educational program (including accredited two-and four-year colleges, universities, vocational-technical and trade schools)

National Young Arts Foundation

Website: https://www.youngarts.org
Social Media: Follow YoungArts on Facebook (https://www.facebook.com/YoungArtsFoundation), X (formerly Twitter) @YoungArts and Instagram @YoungArts
Additional Information: This talent search competition is open to high school students between the ages of 15 and 18 (or in grades 10 through 12) with talent in the arts such as dance, writing, music, theater, visual arts, and jazz. Awards can be used for any field of study. To apply, you must be a citizen or permanent resident of the United States or its official territories (e.g., Puerto Rico). The deadline for final submission is in October. There is an application fee for this program. See the website for details.

Optimist International Oratorical Contest

E-mail: programs@optimist.org
Website: http://www.optimist.org (see *Programs*, then *Scholarship Contests*) or https://www.optimist.org/member/scholarships1.cfm
Additional Information: This scholarship is based on your ability to prepare and present a timed four

to five-minute speech on a specific topic. Contestants, who must be no more than 19 at the time of contest entry, must speak about the official oratorical contest subject, which changes each year. For example, one year's contest subject was "How to Change the World with Optimism." Contest is open to citizens of the United States, Canada, and the Caribbean. You must enter the contest through your local Optimist Club. To locate your local Optimist club, use the e-mail address above. Students must compete in several levels. Visit the website for more details. Award amounts range from $1,000 to $15,000.

NOTE: I competed in the Optimist International Oratorical Contest for several years at various levels beginning in the sixth grade, usually winning at each level but not the final level. Although I did not win the $1,500 award, I did gain invaluable experience in public speaking and in writing speeches, which also helped me to write essays. These are very important skills to have, especially if you want to win scholarships. The ability to speak well in public will help you both in interviews and in preparing essays.

<u>Optimist International Essay Contest</u>

Website: http://www.optimist.org (see *Programs*, then *Scholarship Contests*) or https://www.optimist.org/member/scholarships1.cfm

Additional Information: This is a multilevel essay writing contest. Student winners at the district and international level win scholarships. Contestants must be no more than 19 at the time of contest entry. Contest is open to citizens of the United States, Canada, and the Caribbean. You must enter the contest through your local Optimist Club. To locate your local Optimist club, use the e-mail address above. Visit the website for more details.

Princeton Prize in Race Relations

Website: https://pprize.princeton.edu
Additional Information: The program recognizes and rewards high school students who have had a significant positive effect on race relations in their schools or communities through their volunteer activities. Students can win a $1,000 cash prize. See website for details and to learn about previous recipients.

Profile in Courage Essay Contest

Website: www.jfklibrary.org
Additional Information: In recognition of one of President Kennedy's most important legacies, this contest is designed to promote the involvement of young people in the civic life of their country. High school students in the 9th through 12th grades can

2 – Exploring Scholarships and Awards

participate in this essay contest, by writing a compelling 1000 word (maximum) essay and citing at least five sources on the meaning of political courage. Registration forms must be submitted with the essay and are available on the website. The first place winner and the nominating teacher will be invited to receive awards at the Kennedy Library in Boston. Awards range from $500 to $10,000. The contest deadline is usually in January of each year.

Project Yellow Light Scholarship/Hunter Garner Scholarship

Website: http://projectyellowlight.com
Additional Information: High school and college students who want to encourage fellow students to develop safe driving habits can enter the Project Yellow Light scholarship competition. Your entry, which will consist of a video, billboard design or radio spot designed to motivate, persuade, and encourage your peers not to drive distracted, can win you up to $8,000 for your education. The winning video may be turned into an Ad Council PSA that will be distributed nationally to 1,600 TV stations. The winning billboard design may be displayed on Clear Channel Outdoor digital billboards across the U.S. and the winning radio spot could be shared on iHeartRadio's national network. Visit the website for additional details and requirements.

Scholarships for Average Students

Regeneron International Science and Engineering Fair

Website: https://student.societyforscience.org
Additional Information: Students worldwide in grades 9 through 12 or equivalent, compete in an Intel ISEF affiliated science fair to win the right to attend the Intel ISEF and earn up to $75,000 at Intel ISEF each year.

Scholastic Art & Writing Awards

Website: http://www.artandwriting.org
Additional Information: This program is designed to recognize outstanding talent among students in the visual arts and creative writing. Students submit individual works as well as art portfolios and writing portfolios for this competition. Check the website for entry details in the fall. Awards range from $500 to $10,000.

Shawn Carter Scholarship

Website: https://shawncartersf.com/scholarship
Additional Information: All high school seniors, students with GED diplomas, college undergraduates at two year or four year institutions, and students at vocational or trade schools who are 25 years old or younger can apply for this scholarship. You also need to be a U.S.

citizen and have at least a 2.0 GPA. See website for additional details.
Sodexo Foundation

Sodexo Foundation

Stephen J. Brady STOP Hunger Scholarships
Website:://us.stop-hunger.org/home.html or http://www.sodexofoundation.org (see *Grants and Scholarships*)

Social Media: Follow Sodexo Stop Hunger on Facebook (https://www.facebook.com/SodexoStopHunger) and X (formerly Twitter) @StopHungerUSA. Also see this video of Stop Hunger Scholarship winners and their campaigns on YouTube: https://www.youtube.com/channel/UCzb31RbnB72hY66TwldyBvA

Additional Information: Stephen J. Brady STOP Hunger Scholarships are open to students in kindergarten through graduate school who are enrolled in an accredited educational institution in the United States. The scholarships are available to students who have performed unpaid volunteer services impacting hunger in a community within the United States at least within the last 12 months. Additional consideration is given to students working to fight childhood hunger. A Community Service Recommendation is required for this application form so ask recommenders (who must not be family members) for their recommendations early.

Sons of the American Revolution Joseph S. Rumbaugh Historical Oration Contest

Website: https://www.sar.org (see *Education*)
Additional Information: Oratory competition for high school freshmen, sophomores, juniors, and seniors who submit an original 5 to 6-minute oration on a personality, event, or document of the American Revolutionary War and how it relates to the U.S. today. Oration must be delivered from memory without props or charts. For more information and complete rules, visit the website. Awards range from $200 to $3,000.

Sparkling Ice Flavorful Futures Scholarship Programs

Website: https://www.flavorfulfutures.com
Additional Information: Starting in 2016 through parent company, Talking Rain, this scholarship program has been awarding scholarships to deserving high school seniors throughout the nation. The Flavorful Futures scholarship can be used for part-time or full-time study at any college, university, trade or vocational school. To apply, you must be a graduating high school senior and a U.S. citizen or permanent legal resident of the United States with a cumulative high school grade

point average (GPA) of at least 2.5 on a 4 point scale (high school/homeschooled seniors) and planning to enroll as a freshman or first year student in part-time or full-time study at an accredited two year, four year, college, university, trade or vocational school for the upcoming academic year. A separate and additional scholarship, the Flavorful Futures "Go Green" Scholarship is also available to high school seniors whose educational pursuits are geared towards building a more sustainable future. For the "Go Green" scholarship, you must be planning to pursue a degree related to environmental studies and also provide proof of involvement in sustainable initiatives and projects (volunteer/community service or job) as part of your application.

"Stuck at Prom" Contest

Website: http://www.stuckatprom.com
Additional Information: Contest is open to U.S. citizens who are high school or home-schooled students at least fourteen years of age who create a prom outfit made from Duck-brand duct tape. Although there is no longer a requirement to wear your outfit to the prom, you must submit a photo of yourself in the outfit to enter the competition. You can enter the "Dress" or "Tux" category and submit a color photograph with your entry form and other required documentation. Winners will be

selected based on a variety of criteria, including originality, workmanship, use of Duck tape, use of colors, and creative use of accessories. Award amounts range from $100 to $10,000. Contest begins in late March or early April and ends in early July.

The Christophers Annual Poster Contest for High School Students

Website: https://www.christophers.org/poster-contest
Additional Information: In this yearly contest, students enrolled in the 9th through 12th grades can submit a poster interpreting the theme, "You Can Make a Difference." Prizes range from $100 to $1,000.

"Unboxing Your Life" Video Scholarship

Website: https://www.sttark.com/scholarship/unboxing-your-life-scholarship
Additional Information: Sttark awards a $4,000 scholarship to a U.S. high school senior, undergraduate, or graduate student who is willing to open up and unbox their life in a creative five minute video. To apply for this scholarship, the company wants you to imagine yourself as a carton or box. Then ponder these questions. What would your packaging say? How would you brand

2 – Exploring Scholarships and Awards

yourself? And, most importantly, what story would your box contain? They challenge students to show the contents of their life that make them who they truly are. With your application and video submission, you will also be asked to to submit a brief biography of no more than 250 words.

U.S. Senate Youth Program

The Hearst Foundation
Website: https://ussenateyouth.org
Additional Information: Open to high school juniors or seniors holding a student office. Students must be currently elected to one of the following offices: student body president, vice president, secretary, or treasurer; class president, vice president, secretary, or treasurer; student council representative; or student representative to district, regional, or state-level civic organization. For an application contact your high school principal or state education administrator. Visit the website to find more information about your state's education administrator and the program details. The organization's advice to interested students is to apply in your junior year so that you will have two years of eligibility, rather than one year if you apply as a senior. Award is a $10,000 college scholarship and an all-expense-paid trip to Washington, DC to experience national government in action. Visit the website at the

beginning of your junior or senior year for additional details and current deadlines.

Veterans of Foreign Wars of the United States Voice of Democracy Annual Audio Essay Contest

Website: http://www.vfw.org (Select *Community \ Youth and Education \ Youth Scholarships*)
Additional Information: This scholarship contest is open to grade 9 through 12 students who write and record a three- to five-minute essay addressing the assigned theme, which changes each year. Previous assigned themes have been "I'm Optimistic About Our Nation's Future," "Freedom's Obligation," "Reaching Out to America's Future," and "What Price Freedom?" To participate in this contest, visit the website for more information, speak with your high school counselor, or contact your local VFW post. Scholarship awards range from $1,000 to $30,000. Submissions should go to your local VFW post. Visit the website to find your local post.

3

Easy Scholarships for Lucky Average Students

Often, companies will offer the chance to win cash prizes and scholarships to those who enter their name and contact information in an online sweepstakes. For example, Sallie Mae currently conducts a sweepstakes, offering students thousands of dollars in scholarship awards.

A few search services have drawings similar to a sweepstakes; they may want to obtain your information for marketing purposes but, in return, provide you with a chance to win a scholarship. The primary goal of many companies offering sweepstakes is to get people interested in buying or using their products as they try to win them. In doing so, some offer you a chance to win money for college or other purposes. Once, a website provided the opportunity to win free scholarships all day, every day, just by visiting the site frequently. Following are two examples of scholarship search services:

Scholarships for Average Students

The "No Essay" Scholarship by Niche

Website: https://www.niche.com/colleges/scholarships
Additional Information: Niche offers the "No Essay" Scholarship, which students can enter by simply creating a free profile on their website. No essay or additional documentation is required, making it one of the easiest scholarships to apply for.

$2,000 "Easy" Scholarship by Unigo

Website: https://www.unigo.com/scholarships
Additional Information: Unigo offers a variety of scholarships, including their "$2,000 Easy Scholarship," where students can submit a short entry (often a brief response to a question or prompt). No lengthy essays or forms are required, just a simple submission.

Although these sweepstakes and online lotteries are based almost entirely on luck and the probability of winning can be low, if you have the time and the willpower not to be pulled into buying what you see (you may be bombarded with ads), go for it. But be careful about the information you give and the sites you visit. If it sounds fishy, check it out using the sources in this chapter.

SCHOLARSHIP SCAMS

Since college costs have been escalating higher and higher every year, there are millions of students

3 – Easy Scholarships for Lucky Average Students

and parents who are trying to lessen the cost of their total bill by searching for scholarships. We live in an economy where an easy fix or a promise to reduce the time it takes to do something is a surefire way for people to make money. The scholarship scam artist looks for just the type of person who is trying to reduce the time spent searching for scholarship programs. The following are some typical comments made by scam artists to innocent people in search of scholarship money.

This scholarship requires a handling fee.

A few scholarship programs may ask for a small fee of $5 or less to cover the costs of mailing application materials to you and other administrative costs. To combat this, some scholarship programs may ask that you send an SASE of a certain size to offset the costs of mailing. If a program wants more than this I would be wary of entering, unless it's an artistic competition that may have larger entrance fees. To be safe, contact the Better Business Bureau and your guidance/college counselor or career center director to find out if the scholarship program is legitimate. Most scholarship programs, particularly large ones, do not require either a self-addressed stamped envelope or a handling fee.

We'll do all the work for this scholarship.

All scholarship programs require that you do some type of work, most often some type of essay or entry. When you hear comments like this, remember that all scholarships require you to do something.

You can't get this information anywhere else.

Particularly if the service is touting that it is the only source for a listing of scholarships, more than likely you can get the information in many places for free. Check out:

- The U.S. Department of Education Website (http://www.ed.gov)
- Free computerized scholarship searches such as Fastweb (http://www.fastweb.com)
- The Finaid Website (http://www.finaid.org)
- Books such as *Winning Scholarships for College*—see http://www.scholarshipworkshop.com or ask for it in your local library
- Directories such as *The Ultimate Scholarship Book*
- Your guidance/college counselor or career center director
- Your library
- The college or university you plan to attend
- Social media platforms such as Facebook, Instagram, X (formerly Twitter), YouTube, and more

We need your credit card number or bank account number to hold this scholarship for you.

Never give your or your parents' credit card or bank number to hold a scholarship. Scholarships are

3 – Easy Scholarships for Lucky Average Students

free money. I applied for many scholarships during my search and was never asked, so it would be unusual if you were asked for this information. If I had been, I would have refused to supply it and reported the organization to the Federal Trade Commission.

You have been selected by a "National Foundation" to receive a scholarship, or you have won a scholarship contest when you have never actually applied for the scholarship nor entered the contest.

To win a scholarship from a program you never applied to is virtually unheard of, and if you are told you have won, check out the program by contacting the sources above to see if it is listed anywhere. If it's mentioned in a Web-based source other than that of the federal government, you should not automatically assume it is legitimate. Make sure to contact other sources as well. To be doubly safe, you and your parents should contact the sources in the above section about where you can find information.

We guarantee we'll find at least ten scholarships.

This is a typical line used by many fraudulent scholarship search services. They may also guarantee five or six or some other number. Often the scholarships they are referring to are loan programs, which are not scholarships, or you're ineligible for the scholarships, or you receive the information too late to apply. Refer to the section in this chapter on computerized scholarship search services for more information.

You are eligible to receive a free scholarship and financial aid package. Please call us to schedule your appointment at XYZ Hotel to pick it up.

Usually when you go to pick up your free package at the hotel, you and your parents are subjected to high-pressure sales methods (sometimes about costly insurance programs) meant to make you spend hundreds or thousands of dollars to help you with your scholarship search. The help you receive is something you can usually get from a counselor or by reading a book.

Please attend our free financial aid seminar.

Once again this offer may be an enticement to get you in so you and your parents can be subjected to high-pressure sales methods (often about programs totally unrelated to scholarships) meant to make you spend hundreds or thousands of dollars. The help you receive is something you can usually get from a counselor or by reading a book. Very little information is provided about finding or winning scholarships or getting college financial aid without great cost to you.

4

Earning Scholarships for Activities You Complete, Not Your GPA

As discussed throughout this book, winning scholarships do not always depend on top grades or standardized test scores, as many parents and students think. While it is important to improve your grades, many students may not have an "A" average. They may also not have the highest SAT or ACT score. However, even without them, there are programs that will reward you for different activities you complete that many typical students do as they prepare to hit the college campus in a few months or even a few years. See below for a few examples of these programs.

<u>Cirkled In "No Sweat" Scholarship Program</u>

Website: https://www.cirkledin.com/scholarships
Additional Information: The Cirkled In "No Sweat" Scholarship Program is open to students in grades 8 through 12 in the United States or the District of Columbia. Homeschooled students are also eligible to enter. This scholarship program is designed to make applying for scholarships easy and stress-free so they advertise that no essays or applications are required. Students simply need to create a Cirkled In

Scholarships for Average Students

profile and complete tasks, such as entering achievements and extracurricular activities.

Big Future Scholarship Program

Website: https://bigfuture.collegeboard.org (see Scholarships)

Additional Information: College Board's Big Future Scholarship Program is open to high school students who are making plans to attend college. The program offers numerous opportunities for students to earn scholarships with action steps they take to plan for their collegiate future during their high school years. For example, students can qualify to earn a scholarship (currently $40,000) by completing specific tasks such as exploring colleges, preparing for the SAT, and applying for financial aid. According to the program website, "no essay, no minimum GPA or test score, or citizenship requirements. Just follow the steps for chances to win. The more steps you complete and the earlier you start, the more chances you have to win!"

Raise.me Scholarship Program

Website: https://www.raise.me

Additional Information: The Raise.me Scholarship Program allows high school students to earn micro-scholarships for their achievements during high school. Students can earn scholarships from colleges and universities throughout the country completing activities they are probably already doing such as

4 – Earning Scholarships for Activities You Complete

participating in extracurricular activities, getting involved in community service, or playing a sport. These scholarships are awarded incrementally based on the student's progress and achievements, giving them an early start on funding their college education. To apply for this program, students create a profile on the Raise.me platform and track their accomplishments. The program is open to students in grades 9 through 12. One student I (Marianne Ragins, the author of this book) worked with earned nearly $300,000 in college scholarships using Raise.me. This student started using the program as a high school freshman.

A Student Example

Class Size: 550
Weighted GPA: 3.6
Submitted Test Scores: None. The student was not happy with an ACT score in the low 20's and an SAT score in the low 1000's so chose not to submit.
Common App: Used to submit early action applications for 10 schools. Added the maximum activities allowed for the CommonApp. Included one leadership position (president of a school-based organization). Student also had nearly 200 community serve hours and at least one very strong teacher recommendation.
Merit College Scholarship Total: $476,000 (*had not submitted FAFSA at time of printing for this book*)

5

Searching for Additional Scholarships

Your search should include the following three areas:
- The library
- The Internet
- Local sources: the local search should involve searching for funds available in your community, state, and region.

For a comprehensive search that gives you the best and most opportunities to win scholarship money, devote close attention to all three!

Library Search

To start your scholarship journey, you should go to the nearest library. Once there, do the following:
- Look for scholarship directories such as the *Ultimate Scholarship Book.*
- Search for books such as *Winning Scholarships for College* that go beyond the standard listing found in a scholarship directory. The focus for books of this type is to help you learn how to win scholarships. As a result, they may have limited listings but each listing would include as much additional information on winning the scholarship as possible.

5 – Searching for Additional Scholarships

- Search for newspaper articles about scholarships. Newspapers such as *USA Today* periodically have articles about getting money for college. To find articles in sources like these as well as the magazines above, use the library's online database or microfiche. In addition, an Internet resource you can use would be Google Alerts.

Internet Search

You can use the Internet in many ways to get college information and find the money to pay your way. The example listing in this resource gives you a general summary for many types of programs. If the web page you would like to view is no longer available, try an advanced search on Google because the location may have changed. Or, the competition may have been suspended or discontinued due to lack of funding or a new direction. Unfortunately, this can happen at any time with any program. To help stay informed about new programs, join The Scholarship Workshop on Facebook (www.facebook.com/scholarshipworkshop) or follow us on X (formerly Twitter) @ScholarshipWork for information about new scholarship programs.

Using General Search Engines

Visit search engines such as Yahoo!, Ask, Bing, and Google. Search for terms such as, "college scholarships," "financial aid," and "scholarships." Each of these search engines will give you a list of websites and articles where the term you searched for is included. This will lead you to specific scholarship program websites.

You can also use general search engines to find out if an organization you have heard about in the news or elsewhere has a web address. For example, if a news article lists a program, put the entire name of the program into the search box of an engine with quotation marks around it. By doing this, you may be able to go directly to their website if the search engine finds a link. Or use Google Alerts (www.google.com/alerts) to get e-mail alerts for recent articles written about scholarships, college, and financial aid.

Advanced Internet Search

Have you ever entered a search term in the main search box of a general search engine and received millions of results or advertising pop-ups that really aren't relevant? An advanced search will help you cut through the clutter. You can use the advanced search function in a general search engine such as Google or Yahoo! to find specific information for your scholarship search. An advanced search helps narrow the results you might get from an Internet search.

Perhaps you want to find a scholarship for students with a 2.5 GPA. The example below shows the information you might include for this type of advanced search. Inputting this information into the Google Advanced search uncovered the Regions Riding Forward Scholarship Contest and the Horatio

5 – Searching for Additional Scholarships

Alger National Scholarship Competition among others. You could do a similar search for "3.0 GPA" or another GPA.

Advanced Search		
Find Results	all of these words	national scholarship
	the exact phrase	2.5 GPA
	any of these words	2025 (or current year)
	none of these words	

    Alternatively, you may want to find scholarship contests, awards, or prizes that are based on writing essays. See below for an example of this type of advanced search. Conducting this advanced search can uncover millions of results for essay contests. You could even narrow the results further based on your state or city to find essay based scholarships near you. Also, to eliminate expired competitions, include the current year as well.

Advanced Search		
Find Results	all of these words	scholarship
	the exact phrase	essay
	none of these words	
	any of these words	award or prize or contest

Scholarships for Average Students

Another possible type of advanced search is finding scholarships based on entering drawings that you can win in a sweepstakes or lottery if you are lucky enough to have your name drawn at a specified date and time. Scholarship sweepstakes and lotteries, as discussed earlier in this book, usually do not have a grade component. You don't need to write an essay, be artistic, or participate in any contest based on skill in a particular area. See below for entries to include for this type of search. You can also add the current year in the section with any of these words to include scholarships with upcoming deadlines that have not expired.

Advanced Search		
Find Results	all of these words	scholarship
	the exact phrase	sweepstakes
	none of these words	
	any of these words	

Following is an example including the year. This should help exclude competitions with expired deadlines.

Advanced Search		
Find Results	all of these words	scholarship
	the exact phrase	sweepstakes
	none of these words	
	any of these words	2025

5 – Searching for Additional Scholarships

Alternatively, you could also change your search to look for national scholarships determined in a random drawing.

Advanced Search		
Find Results	all of these words	national scholarship
	the exact phrase	random drawing
	none of these words	
	any of these words	2025

Lastly, another type of scholarship you can search for is one based on submitting a video in a competition. These generally do not have a specific grade requirement either. What would this type of advanced search include? Take a look below for an example.

Advanced Search		
Find Results	all of these words	scholarship
	the exact phrase	video
	none of these words	
	any of these words	award or prize or contest

Local Search

The local search is one most often ignored by the typical student. Usually someone searching for scholarships uses a few scholarship directories and an Internet search service such as www.fastweb.com. For some students in search of college money, an Internet search service is the only resource used. Although search services similar to www.fastweb.com can be wonderful, you should not ignore other sources to find funding. If your scholarship quest includes directories and the Internet only or even just the Internet, you could be overlooking some valuable scholarship opportunities.

The best way to have a complete scholarship search is to search locally in your community, state, and region as well as using directories and the Internet. Most of the scholarships you find in directories and on the Internet are national which means that if you apply, you are among many others who hope to win the scholarship. This makes winning the scholarship harder because it is more competitive. For many local scholarships the number of applications received from students is much smaller which makes them less competitive. This is probably because local scholarships are generally smaller in monetary value and a lot of students feel they aren't worth the time and effort. Fortunately smaller, easier to win scholarships, do add up and should definitely not be ignored. In my scholarship total of more than $400,000, awards as small as $50.00 were included. And my daughter won a small local

5 – Searching for Additional Scholarships

scholarship when she was eight years old in the area where we live.

For a local scholarship search, you should do the following.

- Search for community foundations. Visit the Northern Virginia Community Foundation (www.cfnova.org) for an example of a community foundation and to see types of scholarships a community foundation might have. Visit the Internet search section of this publication to learn how to conduct an advanced search for scholarship information.
- Research local clubs and organizations. Examples of these would be the Soroptimist Club, the Optimist Club, Exchange Clubs of America, Daughters of the American Revolution, YMCA/YWCA, the Kiwanis Club, the Rotary Club, the Lions Club, or the Knights of Columbus. Also look for sororities and fraternities. Optimist International, an organization that has local clubs throughout the country, has an oratorical and an essay contest for students under age 19 where they can win up to $2500 in scholarships. I competed in the oratorical contest for the local Optimist Club in my area over 25 years ago and won quite a few awards in the process. Although I did not win the scholarship, the experience helped to develop many of the communication and writing skills that I have used successfully throughout my life.
- Contact companies and banks located in your community. Some may have scholarships available to local residents. Call the personnel or human resource department of these companies to

Scholarships for Average Students

inquire if they offer scholarships to students in the community.
- Ask your parents to check with their employers. Some employers offer scholarships to children of their employees.
- If your parents belong to a work-related union, contact the union to find out if they offer scholarships to the children of their members. Union Plus is an example of a union that maintains a scholarship program.
- Contact any organization to which you or your parents belong, local or national, to determine whether they have a scholarship program for their members. Your church or faith related organization might be an example.
- Since some credit unions have scholarship opportunities for their members, you should also contact your credit union, if you have one.

6

Applications

For colleges and universities, getting an application is relatively easy. For private organizations and companies, getting an application may require a little more work. However, for some large scholarship programs administered or offered by private companies and organizations, downloading applications from websites and applying online is very popular. Many students prefer applying online because it's quicker and easier. Unfortunately, it's also very easy to make mistakes and to give answers, especially short essay answers, that don't reflect a lot of thought. It is also important to note that if you apply online you can't include most of the winning elements as discussed in the next chapter.

If you absolutely must use an online application, follow these guidelines:
- Print online applications first without completing them
- Complete them on paper
- Then transfer your answers from paper to your computer in the online application
- Print the completed application

Scholarships for Average Students

- Proofread
- If you like everything and have no mistakes, press SEND or whatever button you need to press online to send the application. If you can, make a PDF copy of the applications you complete. This can make it easier to review your application to get ready for a potential interview.

7

Essential Application Tools to Help You Win

What are winning elements? Winning elements are items that set you apart from the crowd when it comes to winning scholarships. Review the following sections for examples of these winning elements.

Essays

Essays are very important to your winning a scholarship. An essay is where you can really shine and tell those who read it how you feel about a particular issue. An essay can help you to elaborate on activities you've outlined in your résumé/activity list. In fact, incorporating your activities, how they have helped to make you into the student or person you are, and how these activities may have helped others, are important features to include in an essay and make its content come alive for the readers, while showing your best qualities.

Résumé/Activity List

Your extracurricular activities, leadership positions, community involvement, and your being a well-rounded student are very important to winning scholarships. To show your involvement in an organized manner with a résumé or an activity list closely resembling a professional résumé helps scholarship programs and educational institutions see your participation and leadership as a whole unit rather than scattered among a few lines on an application.

One of the best ways students can set themselves apart from others is through their extracurricular activities, especially with those that are community service based. Many organizations are very impressed by students who are involved in the community and in their school or educational institution. To show your involvement in an organized and impressive way, you can include a résumé or activity list with your applications. Although most applications will ask you about your activities and include lines for you to list them, your activities look better when presented as a whole and in a résumé-like format. Some students are using the word processing wonders available today to make beautiful résumés complete with pictures and graphic elements that anyone would be proud to show in a job interview. That's the idea. It's great if you have a scholarship judge looking at your résumé/activity list and not only being impressed by what you've done but also

7 – Essential Application Tools to Help You Win

how you presented it. Just make sure you don't overdo it with pictures and graphic elements. Content is the most important factor.

For example, you could organize your résumé in the following manner.

Departmental Clubs/Activities
Here list all activities you are involved in within your school

- *Student Council – 2029 to present* **List activity and years in which you participated**
- *National Beta Club – 2029* **List any positions of leadership held and year held as a subheading **
- *Future Business Leaders of America – 2028 to present*

Honorary Clubs
* List all organizations that you have been inducted into because of outstanding performance *

- *National Honors Society – 2028*

Community Clubs/Service Activities
List clubs or activities within the community

- *Role Models and Leaders Program – 2027 to present*
- *Macon City Volunteer Youth Coach – 2029 to present*
- *NAACP – 2018 to present*
- *Susan G. Komen Race for the Cure – 2028 to present*
- *Community Church Youth Group – 2029 to present*

Work/Internship/Research Experience

- *Laura's Babysitting Services – 2028 to present*

Awards/Honors
*List all the awards you have won.

- *Volleyball Team's Most Valuable Newcomer – 2028*

Scholarships for Average Students

- *Certificate of Participation – Core Advisory Day – 2029*
- *President's Student Service Award – 2028*

*Items in italics <u>and</u> small type are notes to help you create your own résumé.

You can find other types of résumés in *Winning Scholarships for College*. Different formats are acceptable as long as your résumé is easily readable and well-presented.

Recommendations

Another area where students can stand out from the crowd is through the recommendations of others. In order to get the best recommendations you need to be careful about who you ask, how you ask, and when you ask. Here are a few tools to help you do that.

First, consider the scholarship you are applying for. Even if the program is not requesting a recommendation, include one anyway especially if the recommendation is a good one or it highlights your community involvement. On the other hand, if a program specifies no additional documentation be included with your application, respect their wishes.

Nearly all scholarship programs are impressed by those with community involvement. If the program is requesting a recommendation, try to get at least one from an individual that fits the nature of the scholarship. For example, if it's for a STEM (Science, Technology, Engineering and Math) type of scholarship, get your physics, chemistry or another teacher in a related field to write one.

In general, you should get recommendations from the following if you can:
- a teacher
- a counselor or administrator
- a coordinator for a community based activity
- your minister or another clergyman if you have one
- anyone other than a relative who can discuss your most impressive qualities in a written format.

As you think of people to include on your recommendation resource list, make sure to include a sentence about they how they know of you. This will help you to pick and choose individuals to write recommendations as you begin applying for multiple scholarships. Also, when pondering who you should ask, think about whether the person is accustomed to writing recommendations for students or if they might be a good writer. If they have never written a recommendation and/or they aren't a good writer, your recommendation could be a nightmare or a "one liner."

When you ask for a recommendation, do the following:
- Give a written description of the scholarship and/or program
- Include your résumé and any extras you plan to send with your scholarship application

- Include a self-addressed stamped envelope with two stamps (if the recommendation needs to be sent in the U.S. mail)
- Ask at least four weeks before deadline
- Follow-up to see how they are doing or if they need additional information
- Send thank you notes. You may have to ask again.
- *Winning Scholarships for College* (6th edition or later) includes a sample letter requesting a recommendation as well as an example recommendation chart to help you keep track of recommendations and their due dates.

Your Work Samples

If you have done anything extraordinary or award-winning or that has received some type of recognition, include a sample as part of your application package. For example, in my scholarship search, I included an award winning layout from the high school literary magazine where I was the editor. I also included poetry that had won awards as well. In one of my applications, I even included a poem I had written titled, "I Am a Child." I liked the poem and thought it represented my writing style and how I felt about life. It also coincided with my essay where I had written about using my journalism skills (gained through my extracurricular activities) to overcome poverty and destruction in America. The poem which had this line, "I am a child yet I have seen cruelty in the face of kindness," fit the theme of my

7 – Essential Application Tools to Help You Win

application essay. For the essay, I had to answer the question, "You are at your 30th high school reunion. The president of the United States is part of your class. Yet, you are the guest of honor. Why?"

Make sure you don't go overboard when including samples of your work as part of your application package. One or two items you feel are appropriate are enough. Don't send anything that won't fit in a 9" X 11" envelope. And most importantly, if you are asked NOT to send anything extra, DON'T.

Articles

These articles could be on you or your activities (even if the article doesn't mention your name specifically). If you have been a part of an activity or if you started an activity that has been written about in your local newspaper or college newspaper, include a copy of the article. Once again, don't go overboard. One article, if you're also sending samples of your work is enough. Two articles should be your maximum if you're not including samples of your work.

8

Essay Writing Tips to Help Average Students Win

For most essays you can use the following five paragraph format particularly if writing is difficult for you. If writing is one of your strengths, there is no need to follow the five-paragraph format. Just make sure your essay is interesting and includes details about your extracurricular activities and/or your life.

I. INTRODUCTION - ONE PARAGRAPH

- Use a quotation, poem, thought, amazing fact, idea, question, or simple statement to draw your reader into your topic.
- The main idea does not have to be stated in the first sentence, but it should definitely lead to and be related to your main idea or thesis statement, which should introduce three main points you will develop in the body of your essay.
- Avoid using statements such as, "I am going to talk about . . . " or "This essay is about . . ."

II. BODY - THREE PARAGRAPHS

- Support the main idea with facts, thoughts, ideas, published poetry, quotes, and other intriguing, insightful material that will captivate your audience.
- Present clear images.
- If necessary, use a thesaurus to ensure that you are not using the same words repeatedly. Using a word over and over will become monotonous for your audience and distract them from your subject.

III. CONCLUSION - ONE PARAGRAPH

- Restate the main idea in an original way.
- You can again use a poem or quotation to leave an impression. However, avoid using this tactic in all three parts of the essay. It may appear repetitious and unoriginal.
- Refer to the future in terms of your plans pertaining to the subject of your essay. For example, in an essay describing your future career goals, refer to yourself in the career that you have outlined. This reference should project you, and the ideas you presented in the essay, into the future.

* Special Note - Using quotations or poems can show that you are well read. If your essay looks like a dumping ground for quotes and the words of another, using quotations and poems could show something else entirely. Be selective and look for quotes that are enlightening and profound.

As you become more experienced with writing essays you can expand on the format by including more paragraphs or even reducing the number of paragraphs and abandoning the format. If you start with the basic five paragraph format, it is easy to adapt and change to fit the style of your essay, as I did when I wrote an essay for the Coca-Cola scholarship which had nine paragraphs. I also changed the format to write an essay for another scholarship program that had only two paragraphs. You can read both essays and an analysis of each in Chapter 11 of *Winning Scholarships for College*.

Early in your scholarship search, prepare two basic essays following the format above. The essays can easily be tailored later to fit most scholarship application essay requirements.

Since many essays require descriptions of you and your future career goals, let's follow the format to write an essay about you; featuring your activities. In nearly all of the essays I wrote to win scholarships, I incorporated information about specific activities in which I was involved. Once you finish, this essay and parts of it (recycling) can probably be used for every essay you write regardless of the question.

If you have an essay you need to write for a scholarship immediately, it will help if you do the following activities first.

- Finish your résumé/activity list if you haven't already. This needs to be done before you begin any essay. Using the information from your résumé/activity list, you should include additional details about your activities to support the main points of your essay. Scholarship organizations are very impressed by students who are involved in various endeavors beyond typical classroom work. Showing your passion and commitment to certain activities by including more information about your involvement will help you stand out from the crowd of other applicants. Refer to the chapter, "Grades Don't Mean Everything," in *Winning Scholarships for College* for more information and also the "Essential Application Tools to Help You Win" chapter in this publication.

- Research the organization or company sponsoring the scholarship or award.
- Learn why the scholarship was established and the mission of the organization. If one or more of your activities fit the reasoning behind why the scholarship was established or the organization's mission you may want to highlight this in your essay.
- Understand the question. Think of several ways you might answer and write them down.
- Look at the scholarship application. What do most of the questions focus on: academics, community involvement, etc.? If an organization asks most of its application questions about community involvement, then try to build your essay around activities you do that benefit the community.

Since you are writing a descriptive essay about you or your future career goals, featuring your activities, the next step is to think of three adjectives that describe you. For each adjective, write down an activity that fits with that adjective.

For example, the five paragraph essay format would now look like the following:

I. INTRODUCTION - ONE PARAGRAPH
  A. Adjective/Noun 1
  B. Adjective/Noun 2
  C. Adjective/Noun 3

II. BODY - THREE PARAGRAPHS

  A. Adjective/Noun 1
  1. Activity 1
  2. Activity 2
  3. Activity 3

  B. Adjective/Noun 2
  1. Activity 1
  2. Activity 2
  3. Activity 3

  C. Adjective/Noun 3
  1. Activity 1
  2. Activity 2
  3. Activity 3

Note: You do not need three activities for each. If you have only two, that's okay.

III. CONCLUSION - ONE PARAGRAPH
  A. Summarize your adjectives and how they relate to you and your activities. Refer to the future.

As you write about activities in your essay, don't just list them as you did with your résumé/activity list. If you do, the essay is really saying nothing more than you already did. When you write about your activities, you should be answering these questions as part of your essay:

1. What is the activity?
2. Who does the activity benefit?
3. When do you participate in this activity?
4. Where do you participate in this activity?
5. How does this activity benefit you or others?
6. Why are you involved in the activity?

Based on the outline, adjectives, activities, and answers to the above questions, you could begin your essay like the example below, assuming the adjectives you chose were self-motivated, energetic, and compassionate:

When I think of the words self-motivated, energetic, and compassionate, I think of myself. For the past seven years, starting in elementary, into middle school and now my first two years in high school, I have participated in many activities that reflect these words. More than just words, they really describe who I am and how I feel about life.

For example, in terms of self-motivation, I built a website and Facebook page for students interested in getting tutors at our middle school and continued maintaining it during high school. Building the website and populating it with insightful content was a frustrating and challenging task I set for myself. It took me most of the summer before my freshman year at XYZ High School, but I finished it to the amazement of my parents and friends. The website, once completed, became a much-needed reference for students in our community to find tutors and other information to help them in all types of subjects. The website also helped the upper-class students who became tutors make a little money to get a jump-start on college expenses. Most importantly, for those who weren't interested in charging, the site helped those who just wanted to aid their peers and apply principles they learned in class.

As a freshman at XYZ High School, I began to show more of my energetic traits by participating in several athletic activities concurrently which really challenged my self-motivation and determination, but most importantly helped me to relearn the value of teamwork and cooperation for all endeavors. I joined the volleyball team. I became a varsity cheerleader . . .

The next paragraph would focus on compassionate. The last paragraph would be a summary and conclusion. This essay is an example of a rough draft for a descriptive essay using the adjectives self-motivated, energetic, and compassionate. It still needs work but it's meant to give you an idea of how to structure your essay using the adjectives or nouns you selected and the examples of your activities that could fit the adjectives or nouns you selected.

To get additional information about planning your essays, choosing adjectives, writing about your activities, and writing different types of essays, read *The Scholarship & College Essay Planning Kit*.

9

Scholarships Hacks and Mistakes To Avoid

The following includes a list of hacks you should know to help you win scholarship money. It also includes some mistakes that could reduce your chances of securing money for college.

- If you're a high school senior, use the Common App and apply early action to colleges and universities that interest you. With early action acceptance from colleges and universities, you may also receive scholarship offers with your congratulatory letters. Do not apply for the binding early decision. Just apply by the early action application deadline. More specifically, early decision plans are binding: A student accepted under early decision must attend the college. Alternatively, early action decisions are not binding. Although you may receive an early response to your application, you do not have to commit to the college until the typical decision date of May 1.
- Use an appropriate e-mail address. For example: firstnamelast name@xyz.com. Your address can give a negative or positive impression of you. It's amazing how much little things can matter.

For example, an e-mail address such as imanidiot@aol.com, ilovemyboyfriend@xyz.com, or ihatewomen@gmail.com is certainly not appropriate.

- Check your e-mail. Even if you have more than one e-mail address, have your e-mails forwarded to the account you check daily. Some providers still send letters in the mail but many now send e-mails and potentially texts for initial acceptance and notifications. Don't miss an opportunity because you don't regularly check e-mail.
- Use a professional username and password. Slang words or derogatory names as a username or password do not present a professional image. You should assume that any information you submit can be seen by anyone (this includes via Facebook, X (formerly Twitter), Instagram and other social media). If you want something to stay private, do not submit or transmit it. This includes personal information. And always be aware of the words you post online and how they might appear to others, especially if you want them to contribute to funding your education. Naming you as a scholar or winner of their award means you are their representative. If they feel you will not present a positive image for their organization, they will not want to select you as a winner.
- Spell-check, grammar-check, and have someone else check your work so you can make the best first impression.
- Understand that with many national programs, the application pool has increased significantly.

9 – Scholarship Hacks and Mistakes to Avoid

What does this mean to you? Be competitive. Extracurricular activities, community service, and leadership are key. And make sure to apply for local and regional scholarships as well, where you may be competing against fewer than a couple-dozen applicants.

- Use your essays to tell the rest of your story that application questions don't address. Do not give a laundry list of activities that are revealed elsewhere in your applications. Expand upon your activities by answering the questions: Who? What? When? Where? How? and most important, Why? as it relates to an activity.
- Choose someone to recommend you who will be able to answer questions about you from a personal and academic perspective.
- Clean up your social media life. If your name and information is on a Facebook page, X (formerly Twitter), Instagram account, or YouTube video with derogatory, unflattering, or inflammatory remarks or visuals, you need to do some immediate clean up. Although many outside scholarship programs may not have the time to look you up on social media, some programs might and many universities and colleges do, particularly if considering whether to award one of the most prestigious scholarships they have to offer to you.
- Do not answer questions on applications or in any written communication in the form of text language.
- Do not wait until the last minute to start or complete an online application. According to most scholarship providers, online applications

are the norm. However, some online application programs can have technical issues when the system becomes overwhelmed near the deadline as masses of students apply. Apply at least a week before the deadline date if you can.
- Do not use abbreviations or slang in your answers. It can create an unprofessional impression of you and your achievements.
- Do not indicate anywhere in your essay that you are reusing the same essay you wrote for another competition, even if you are recycling an essay. Although many organizations understand that the scholarship search and win process can be exhausting and time consuming, they still prefer essay answers that are crafted specifically for their award or scholarship.
- Do not use ChatGPT or artificial intelligence (AI) to write your scholarship and college essays. Remember, "if it sounds too good to be true, it probably is." Essays generated by artificial intelligence often contain inauthentic and inaccurate information that sounds totally unlike you or any other teenager or college student. Although it's easy to get the help of AI, using it to generate your essay may hurt your chances. Just like experts who read college and scholarship essays can determine a parent wrote a student's essay, they can often tell when AI generates an essay.

10

Other Strategies to Reduce Your Tuition Bills

The following information includes a host of strategies you can use to cut your tuition bill as an middle class student.

- Go to a community college for the first two years. This should cost significantly less than a four-year institution, particularly if you live at home. Using this strategy could potentially get you a degree from an expensive and possibly prestigious institution at a fraction of the cost. If you decide to do this, make sure the courses you take during your first two years will transfer to the four-year school you want to attend and that they will count toward your bachelor's degree.
- If you're interested, consider certain majors in science, technology, engineering, or mathematics (STEM) related fields. These fields usually have more scholarship money available to them than others.
- If you can do it without completely exhausting yourself, consider completing four years of

undergraduate work in three. Or, make sure you finish in four years instead of five or six years.
- Look at institutions that have a matching grant system. In this system if a student who enrolls has an outside scholarship, the institution may match the amount of the outside scholarships up to a certain amount.
- Research and look at schools that value your interests. For example, if you are considering an unusual major in which a college or university may be starting a department, you may be able to get a scholarship or reduced tuition from them as they begin looking for students to enroll in their new program.
- Look at universities and colleges where your grades and SAT scores will place you in the top 10 to 25 percent of prospective students. To find this information, consult a guide such as *Peterson's Four-Year Colleges* to find statistics such as these for the freshman class and student body. If your grades and SAT scores are in the top tier of the students the school tries to attract, you have a good chance of securing more aid from the school.
- Consider participating in the AmeriCorps program or a similar program, which allows participants to earn education awards or scholarships in return for some type of service or employment during or after college. For more information about service scholarships,

10 – Other Strategies to Reduce Your Tuition Bills

review chapter 14 of *Winning Scholarships for College*, "Scholarships & Awards for Community Service, Volunteering and Work."
- Consider the military as an option to reduce your costs. The U.S. armed forces offer several educational programs:
    o You can attend one of the military academies. If you are accepted to a military academy you can essentially go to college for four years tuition-free while earning a commission.
    o You can enroll in the Reserve Officers Training Corps (ROTC) program while in college. ROTC will pay for your tuition, fees, and books and may provide you with a monthly allowance.
    o You can join the armed forces before you go to a college and use the Montgomery GI Bill to help pay for college expenses once you've completed your military service.
    o In some instances, you can earn college credit for certain military training. This could possibly reduce the number of classes you'll have to take in college.

11

Using Crowdfunding to Get Money for College

Crowdfunding allows students to tell their story over the Internet to thousands of people quickly and with minimal effort. Individuals all over the world with access to the Internet see a student's words and hopefully become compelled to contribute with funding. There are several popular crowdfunding sites such as www.gofundme.com or www.gogetfunding.com.

Following are some tips for a successful crowdfunding campaign:
- You should have great visuals. If you can take a picture of yourself with something from your future college or university, like a sign or mascot, it might help to encourage alumni and others to donate because it may give them an immediate visual connection with you.
- Use social media. Let others know about your campaign on your social media accounts but ask ALL of your family members with active social media accounts

11 – Using Crowdfunding

to share. If you attend a church or faith based organization, ask them to share on their social media. Also contact the youth and young adult ministry, scholarship ministry, education ministry and similar ministries to let them know about your campaign.
- Don't forget to create a hashtag specific to your campaign. This can make it easier to follow your campaign and see the interest it's getting.
- Check with your current or future university to see how you can connect with alumni via social media, email, or another way to share your campaign. Also check out the web site and social media accounts for the alumni association in your hometown.
- Give a compelling and interesting name to your campaign. It should be something that people can easily remember. For example, Amy Needs Your Dollars for College - I Could Be Your Future Physician.
- Post updates. Let people know how it's going for you. Share success and failure. And let them know how much you appreciate the money already contributed and how wonderful it will be when you reach your campaign goal. You might also share what you've done with money contributed so far.

Scholarships for Average Students

- Offer an incentive. You could offer something like a free hour of live or web based tutoring for one student at the local high school or middle school for every $100 or $1000 you receive. Or you could offer to spread the love by helping at a food bank, a shelter or some other community organization one hour per month every time you reach a $1000 threshold (or some other number) in your campaign.
- In your story, share your future career plans and how you plan to help others in the future just like donors will hopefully help you now. For example, you could discuss setting up a mentoring program or joining an organization such as Big Brothers Big Sisters once you graduate. Or for those with family members affiliated with a Greek organization mention future participation in the community service efforts of those organizations (if you successfully pledge).
- Let donors know exactly how the money will be used. For example: I need $5,000 for my room and board deposit at XYZ university. Or indicate the money is for next semester's tuition payment.
- Consider adding a video to your story. Something memorable would be best. People love videos with animals. Maybe include your favorite pet in a video saying how much you will miss him or her doing

11 – Using Crowdfunding

their favorite stunt while you're away at college. But you're planning for a great future for both of you in your own home after you graduate. Or perhaps the video could be of you showcasing a special skill or talent you plan to share with others as a future college student or graduate.

Crowdfunding is a great way to raise last minute cash for school. However, your funding campaign may not raise as much as you want or need. You should make every effort to explore additional sources of funding explained in other sections of this guide. Also don't forget to explore scholarships, grants and awards for current college students. Don't stop looking for additional funding until all your current and future college bills are fully funded.

www.ingramcontent.com/pod-product-compliance
Lightning Source LLC
Chambersburg PA
CBHW050039080526
44586CB00014B/1380